BROWN EYED GIRL: A JOURNEY TO SELF-LOVE

Michae' Wiley-Edgecombe' PhD

Brown Eyed Girl Copyright © 2021 by Michae' Wiley-Edgecombe' PhD. All Rights Reserved.

No part of this book may be reproduced in any form or by any electronic or mechanical means including information storage and retrieval systems, without permission in writing from the author. The only exception is by a reviewer, who may quote short excerpts in a review.

Please note that all story times are historical fiction. This means that they are based on true events, however, are not specific to any one individual's journey.

Cover designed by Justin Carey Designs

Printed in the United States of America
First Printing: October 2021
The Scribe Tribe Publishing Group

THE SCRIBE TRIBE
PUBLISHING GROUP

ISBN-978-1-7376411-1-7

Acknowledgements

Throughout my life, I have been blessed to have been surrounded by many positive individuals.

It is my belief that all these positive influences have impacted me professionally and personally.

It is impossible to list all these individuals and experiences. So, friends, family, and well-wishers, I thank you.

Professionally, I have worked with many women of color.
I am very proud to have witnessed your growth.
I acknowledge all of you and applaud you on your journey.

Contents

1: *Dear Black Girl* — 6
2: *What is Love?* — 10
3: *To Thy Self Be True* — 18
4: *Be Kind to Yourself* — 26
5: *Protect Yourself* — 35
6: *Cleaning House* — 42
7: *Celebrate the Small Wins* — 47
8: *Dating & Loving You* — 52
9: *Treat Yourself Like Someone You Love* — 56
About the Author — 67

*"How can you appreciate the sun if you've never felt the rain?
How can you grow flowers if you're afraid to put your hands in the dirt?
How can you appreciate the springtime if you've never felt the winter's cold?"*
-Essie Henry Wiley

Chapter 1: Dear Black Girl

As Black and brown girls, we are taught that we must always be our best selves. We feel as though our families, communities, and society place us under a microscope examining and dissecting our every move. Fun fact: Black American women are the highest educated population in America.

As Black women, we wear many hats. We are sisters, daughters, mothers, partners, wives, executives, breadwinners, etc. In these roles we feel that we must do so with a smile. We face life's hurdles fearlessly and non-threatening at the same time.

While trying to break through the many glass ceilings placed in front of us, we are taught to do so while exhibiting the strength of our ancestors. We barely break a sweat, let alone shed a tear. We are taught to make our struggles look easy. While pounding the cement pavement, we must remain perfectly manicured with sparkling Colgate smiles. If we make one wrong move we are viewed as weak, prideful, or worse, the angry Black woman.

All this sounds somewhat negative however, let's truly examine our strength. Our smiles serve as a glimmer of hope in what for others may feel like a hopeless situation. Our smiles serve as a commitment to ourselves that greater is coming. As we face the many complexities of life, our smiles provide hope to our families, communities, as well as ourselves.

Our well-manicured hands, groomed hair, and polished appearances provide a sense of self-worth and self-love. We could look like we feel but as Black women, we choose to look the way we are striving to feel, if that makes sense. I'm not saying spend your life's savings on your appearance; I'm simply explaining why we always look the part.

The angry Black woman is a concept that is meant to be viewed as a negative. However, in most cases, the angry Black woman is simply a passionate woman striving for her personal best. The angry Black woman oftentimes is simply a passionate woman who refuses to settle for less. She speaks her truth. Others may not be able to accept her truth, thus framing her as angry instead of passionate.

I challenge Black women to be strong enough to feel. What does that mean and why? Being strong enough to feel means being strong enough to identify how you truly feel in each moment. Examine those feelings and create an agenda on how to conquer those emotions.

I also challenge Black women to be each other's support system. Supporting each other can be a superpower. Listen to each other and build each other up. We are not each other's competition. We are our sister's keeper.

No one said that being a Black woman was easy. Due to cultural circumstances, we are taught to "lay it on the altar" or "let it go." While spiritual connections are a key component to happiness, many of us have not been provided the tools necessary to just "let it go."

The goal of this book is to examine love, self-worth, and self-love. While examining these concepts, you will be provided with mini exercises that are designed to help build self-love and assist you on your journey to loving the person that you are.

Before we go any further I'd like to take this time to validate you as a Black woman. Although the world may vigorously challenge you, you are powerful, strong, and good enough simply because you are you. Without one change, you are valuable. Without one ounce of make-up, you are beautiful. And yes, even in your bonnet, you are amazing. Although times you may not feel worthy, your tears matter, your laughter changes the world, and your fight is not in vain. This book in no way means to offend. Yes, it will be hard and yes, it will be worth it.

I love the concept of Black girl magic. However, to achieve Black girl magic the first step is self-love. I hope that you are blessed by this next chapter. Buckle up let's begin your journey!

You is smart.
You is kind.
You is important.
-The Help

Pieces of Me Exercise:

Please take this time to discover yourself. Who are you? Look at you in terms of a puzzle. What are the many pieces of you?
(i.e., wife, mother, friend, baker, writer, coach, encourager, etc.)

Self-reflection can be difficult. Take your time to really look at who you are. As you look at the woman staring back at you, ask yourself what you wish to accomplish by working through this workbook.

_____
_____
_____
_____
_____
_____

Chapter 2: What is Love?

When reading the title to this chapter, many of you familiar with tunes from the 80's or 90's instantly heard a song playing in your head. If you moved your head from left to right in a semi head-banging motion, I'll finish the sentence for you... *"Baby, don't hurt me."* For those who didn't, YouTube it and you'll get a great laugh. I promise.

In all seriousness, we need to answer this question. How can we embark on this journey if we have no idea what love is? I believe that many of us lack a proper understanding of love therefore, we are unable to achieve it for ourselves.

The biblical definition provided in the King James Version of the Bible is found in 1st Corinthians.

Love is patient, love is kind. It does not envy, it does not boast, it is not proud. It does not dishonor others, it is not self-seeking, it is not easily angered, it keeps no record of wrongs. Love does not delight in evil but rejoices with the truth. It always protects, always trusts always hopes, and always perseveres. Love never fails. But where there are prophecies, they will cease; where there are tongues, they will be stilled; where there is knowledge, it will pass away. For we know in part and we prophesy in part, but when completeness comes, what is in part disappears. When I was a child, I talked like a child, I thought like a child, I reasoned like a child. When I became a man, I put the ways of childhood behind me. For now, we see only a reflection as in a mirror; then we shall see face to face. Now I know in part; then I shall know fully, even as I am fully known. And now these three remain: faith, hope, and love. But the greatest of these is love. -1 Corinthians 4:13

My interpretation of this scripture is that love makes you feel good. This "feel good" experience evokes positive feelings: mentally, emotionally, spiritually, and physically. Each of these areas of "the feel-good experience" will be discussed within the pages of this book. It is important to think of self-help as a journey which encompasses all components of life. For example, it is hard to have overall joy when ignoring your mind, body, or soul.

My favorite definition of love comes from Dr. Maya Angelou's 2011 interview with Oprah Winfrey. Her definition is as follows:

"Love. And again, see I don't mean, I think love is that condition in the human spirit so profound, that it allows us to forgive, and it may be the energy which keeps the stars in the firmament, I'm not sure. It may be the energy which keeps the blood running smoothly through our veins. I'm not sure, but it's something beyond the explanation. It can be used for anything you can explain. Any good thing you can explain." — Maya Angelou

Love is complex. Researchers have been studying the complexities of love for centuries. They try to answer the questions, "What is love?" and "What makes us fall in love and why?" Researchers have defined love as a variety of feelings, states, and attitudes that vary from interpersonal affection to pleasure. However, it is so much more.

The desire to be loved is a natural human desire. As humans, our desire to be loved arises in infancy. As infants, we develop attachments to our caregivers. Attachments in infancy are the emotional bonds that children develop with those providing care for them. It is natural to wish to feel safe, secure, and unconditionally loved.

In the English language, love is both a noun and a verb. Let's take a journey back to 3rd grade, shall we? A noun is a word, other than a pronoun, used to identify a person place or thing.

As a noun love is a tender, passionate affection for another person. A feeling of warm personal attachment or deep affection. *Used in a sentence: He is the love of my life.*

A verb is a term used to show action or a state of being. As a verb love is defined as the act of having love or affection for someone or something. *Used in a sentence: I love coffee.*

After working on yourself, I'd love this sentence to eventually read, I love me.

To avoid confusion lets briefly discuss what love isn't. Love is not:
- A transaction or subjective—you should not have to do things from others to receive love.
- A game—love should not keep score. Keeping a score only builds resentment.
- Have limits—there are no limits to love.

Many of us are led to believe that love is transactional. Transactional love means that if we do something then we deserve to be loved. Within dating experiences, we believe that if we act a certain way, wear the right clothing, or cook the right meal, our loves will love us back. Wrong! Genuine love requires nothing.

Many of us require transactional love from ourselves; this notion concerns me even more than transactional love from others. Think back to the last time you were on a diet or had an educational goal. Keep thinking, I'll wait... We often time say things like, "After I loose these 10, 20, 80 pounds, I'll start feeling better about me." What happens if you do all the Keto, Weight Watchers or intermittent fasting in the world and the scale never changes? Does this mean that you won't began your journey to self-love?

Many of us Black women do this with education or career goals. "Once I'm the head of the company or earn that degree, I'll start loving me more." But once we climb those mountains, we only find more mountains to climb.

Story Time: Wanna hear it? Here it Go!

I came from a family where education was important. My dad constantly said, "Your knowledge is the only thing that man can't take from you." He was definitely right. However, the way I viewed education became the way I valued myself. When I graduated high school, I was at the top of my class. I earned two bachelor's degrees at the same time while others struggled to attain one. I received my master's degree free of charge through academic scholarship. With each of those degrees, I felt nothing. I still didn't see myself as being good enough. So, I embarked upon my doctoral studies. I thought that maybe if I was able to become Dr. Wiley then the world would respect me. But most importantly, I thought I'd respect me. I thought that I'd finally feel worth it.

During my doctoral studies, I took my coursework very seriously and sailed through the course work portion of my degree. *Piece of cake,* I thought to myself. I only received one 'B', and I just knew that it was because my professor was hating on me.

When I hit the dissertation phase of my studies, the bottom dropped out of my life. Yes, the work was stressful, overwhelming, and intense. For the first time in the history of Michae, I felt educationally defeated. I felt like I was not smarter than a 5th grader. Every sentence I wrote was criticized. Yes, the woman who wrote papers in her sleep, edited papers for colleagues, and wrote entire training manuals.

One day I was in my room dancing the bachata with my then boyfriend (now husband). One minute I was dancing and the next I was unable to move. I was too embarrassed to call for help. I just needed to pull myself together is what I told myself. Wow! Just days after making my first defense to receive Institutional Review Board (IRB) approval, I suffered 2 strokes. Yep, not one but two! Michae' never does anything halfway—not even sickness.

I suffered brief paralysis on the left side of my body and other physical symptoms. I couldn't speak for a few hours. All I remember thinking was who would care for my daughter. I didn't care about a degree, a dissertation or doctor anything. All I wanted was for my one true love to be well taken care of.

Yes, I finished my degree, but not without stress. My strokes caused short-term memory loss. So, climbing the mountain took twice as long. I finished my educational journey for my daughter for me to provide the life I envisioned for her.

My desire to complete my doctoral degree helped me to see that love is not a game. We should never flip a coin to decide if we love ourselves. Nor should we quantify our love for ourselves and others based on something other than just pure love.

I asked this question of twenty Black women from all walks of life. While many did not respond, the responses that I received back were amazing.

I used the following script: *I'm conducting research on how Black women view self-love. Your feedback is appreciated. Please note: no identifying information will be shared in any publication. In your own words, please define self-love. Is self-love important to you as a Black woman?*

1st Response
Self-love is making sure your mental, spiritual, and physical being is taken care of regardless of what's going on around you. Self-love is knowing it is absolutely okay to put yourself first sometimes. Self-love is not allowing anyone to disrupt your peace no matter who they are. Self-love is important to me as a Black Woman, and I attribute a huge part of the love I pour into me from keeping me from falling into depression.

2nd Response (15-year-old girl)

As a young Black woman self-love is very important to me. I was taught at a very young age it was important to love yourself, because if you didn't love yourself and put yourself first then no one else would. As being a young Black woman, society treats us as less than anyone else in the world. We are portrayed as the lowest of the low, yet we are the strongest beings on earth, and we constantly have things stolen from us. I have always felt that since society won't love us or treat us the way that we should be treated than it is important for us to love ourselves. To hold ourselves with grace and dignity and to know that we are worthy of being loved and of having love. But first we must love ourselves and come to acceptance with who we are.

3rd Response

To me, self-love is loving and living for yourself in the ultimate way. Self-love is important as a Black woman because we are often not able to give ourselves self-love. Black women often are not taught to have a voice for themselves. I feel if we were able to have a voice for ourselves, a lot of things would be different in society. We are not guaranteed the opportunities like others because of the color of our skin. Additionally, as a Black woman, it's so much competition with each other especially with social media. Women of color are always at each other because of the way they dress, the way they wear their hair, and many other things. Often, Black women are known for a lot of negative things that would make any young or older female feel unattractive or unworthy just for being Black. I feel it's important to have self-love to be able to change barriers and make a difference with other women that are going through similar challenges.

4th Response

Self-love is something I am still struggling to understand and execute daily. I see it as self-care and taking time for myself and putting my needs over the needs of others at times. It is very important to me to have time for self and to love myself with the same energy as I love others.

5th Response

Self-love is taking care of yourself mind, body, and soul. It is making sure the woman in the mirror is great! Yes, I think it's important because you can't love anyone else if you don't love yourself.

6th Response

As a Black woman self-love is everything. It wasn't until recently that I realized for many years I have not been loving me correctly. I've lived in the shadows of the woman I want to be and still am becoming. I lived a life filled with what others wanted me to be or who they thought I was. I've missed out on so much exploration and living because I was afraid and didn't really understand that I only get one life and I should love myself enough to live it.

I'm really in a place in my life now where I'm learning to love and appreciate me, the good the bad and the ugly. And I'm loving me through every painful experience enough to make me better. I'm loving me through every failure in my life.

7th Response

Self-love is making sure that the choices you make are making you happy. Self-love is so important as Black women. We have had to fight to prove we are an equal counterpart to men and have been put down for so many years. So, it is important to know how to love ourselves and be confident in who we are. We must make daily affirmations that we are enough despite what the world says or thinks.

8th Response

Self-love can be described as a basic human necessity and as a selfish flaw. For me, self-love is a human necessity and something I wish I made more of a routine. Self-love can be whatever makes you feel good, brings you happiness and gives you the strength to keep going on with life. Monthly massages, hair appointments, yoga, shopping, reading, praying, or anything that revitalizes your soul.

9th Response

As a Black woman self-love is extremely important because I tend to take on the world and doing so can be physically and emotionally exhausting. Sometimes, I make my family my world. I take on their sadness, fears, anxiety, happiness, and stress. Everything they go through, I go through. So, making time for myself love is extremely important.

10th Response

My interpretation is having the ability to accept God-given grace and peace to my own person- to forgive myself and overcome my personal shortcomings that I become able to follow God's mandate to impart love and forgiveness to others. Without self-love, one has not the ability to love thy neighbor.

11th Response
My definition of self-love is to respect honor and love yourself like only you can. Taking care of yourself includes physical, mental, and spiritual care. As a Black woman this gets hard to do as I often feel the weight of the world on my shoulders. When this occurs, I must block out the world's pressures and really invest in myself.

Let's look at the trends that were established in this data. Eleven responses are stated here due to data saturation. Not to sound like a researcher, (although I really am one), but data saturation briefly defined is the point in qualitative research when "no new information or themes are observed in the data."

Trend	Present in Response	Not Present
Self-care	11	N/A
Setting self as a priority	11	N/A
Caring for your mental health	7	4
Caring for your spiritual health	7	4
Caring for physical health	5	4
Not competing	9	2
Ignoring outside or societal pressures	8	3
Unconditional love	9	2

Now let's define self-love in the eyes of Black women. Self-love is the act of caring for yourself without conditions regardless of societal standards and pressures. Self-love is taking care of your own mind, body, and soul in efforts to become your best self. Self-love consists of taking the time, efforts, and energy to strengthen yourself in all areas that concern you. It's loving yourself just as you would love someone else.

For the sake of this correspondence, we will define love as a virtue (behavior showing a moral standard) representing human kindness, compassion, and affection.

Love is:
- Objective – Its value is something that is outside of the item. An example is loving someone for who they are.
- An action – Remember love is a verb; it shows action or being. The word alone is simply a word.
- Truth – It provides honesty. While many say love does not hurt, the truth is a component of love in that one must provide the truth to genuinely love someone.
- Authentic – Love is unconditional. Love does not come with any buts. One must love and accept the person for who they are.
- Forgiveness – The act of love comes with one's willingness to forgive to grow.
- Growth – Love provides an understanding that provides nurturing, which will render growth.

What is Love?

Although I have shared how love is defined in the English language to researchers and poets as well as myself, I have a challenge for you. Take your time and answer the question for yourself. What is love?

_____
_____
_____
_____
_____
_____
_____
_____
_____
_____
_____
_____
_____

Chapter 3: To Thy Self Be True:
Examining Self-Worth and Self-Love

This chapter is personally challenging for me as a Black woman. Growing up in the skin that I am in was overwhelming. Let's draw a picture of Michae'. Take out your imaginary pen and pad, please. As a woman, I stand 5-foot, 1-inch tall. My skin is the color of a latte. My hair is shoulder length however, in its most natural state, it may reach my ear (when my curls are popping). I'm 150 pounds. I have relatively large breasts and if I stood against a wall my back and legs would lay even against it (meaning my butt is missing, like it is invisible). Growing up, I usually wore a shirt and tie. I felt like the tie would force people to take me more seriously. I ultimately felt that wearing additional clothing covered my breast. Thus, taking the attention from my breast and onto me as a person. These days I am known for my colorful sweater dresses. They still cover my breasts and I wear something to make sure I show no cleavage, like ever. I speak the King's English and take pride in my education. I am self-made, which is a nice way of saying I work my butt off. (Maybe this explains the lack of behind!) It took me years to love the picture of me that I am today.

Growing up I heard things like "baldhead bougie girl." Or people saying, "You think you are all of that." Family members called me fat. I was told that I sound white or that I wanted to be a white girl. Heck, I've even been called even worse. I'd look at myself wishing I was anyone else but me. I made several attempts to avoid being the person that I am. I dieted so much that you could see my ribs. I'd limit myself to one meal per day. I relaxed my hair so much that I forgot what my curls looked like. I used slang that didn't even sound anything like English. Don't get me started on the weaves, wigs, and fake ponytails. I didn't stop relaxing my hair or wearing wigs and weaves (other than braids) until my then 5-year-old asked me not to braid her hair because she "loved her Afro hair." She's 15 now. It took for my child to teach me, *a well-educated woman*, to love her hair.

Women, in general, are given an overwhelming standard of beauty and prestige by society. Aesthetically, women must be fair-skinned, thin, have long flowing hair, maintain just the right style, and have a body that is pleasing to the eye. Personality-wise, society believes that women must be patient, kind, soft, and loyal. That standard is difficult for any woman to achieve. I believe that's why the beauty industry is a billion-dollar machine in America.

Now add the component of being a Black woman into the mix. Society sets a standard of beauty that is naturally unattainable for most Black women. Our skin varies in color. Our hair has kinks and curls, and we have our own sense of what's stylish. Our bodies have curves that have been given to us by our ancestors. From day one, we come out the womb feeling less than. Many Black women spend the rest of their lives living up to a standard of beauty that is not ours.

The personality standards set for women in America is also unreachable for Black women. Stereotypically, Black women are seen as loud, demanding, and boisterous. Now, remember this is a stereotype. We may have some of those qualities, however these qualities are positive rather than negative. As Black women, we play different roles culturally within our communities. As Black women, many of us lead our families. For many of us, our grandmothers served as leaders of our families no matter how functional or dysfunctional. Typically, the backbone to most Black families is a wise grandmother or great-grandmother who is behind the scenes guiding and directing the family. She had wise words and structure that demanded attention and kept the family afloat. For this reason, Black women can't always be soft.

Brief history lesson: During the enslavement of Black people in America, not only did Black females have a job on the plantation, but they also took care of the Black children. Heck, they even cared for the white children. Many Black male slaves were sold off and families were torn apart, thus leaving the female slaves to take care of what was left of the family. The strength of the Black woman is deeply rooted. She had to be hardworking to take care of her family, loud to be heard, and be fearless to withstand the pressures placed upon her. So, the second step in this journey is to re-define your standards of beauty based on true beauty, not societal beauty.

Re-Defining Standards of Beauty Exercise:

For this next exercise it is required that you remove the societal blinders and look at the beautiful human that you are.

What makes you unique as a Black woman?
_____
_____
_____
_____

What is your favorite physical component of yourself?
_____
_____
_____
_____

What are you most proud of as related to being melanated?
_____
_____
_____
_____

What do you love best about your hair?

_____

_____

_____

_____

What do you like best about your skin?

_____

_____

_____

_____

When you look in the mirror what's the first thing you notice about yourself?

_____

_____

_____

_____

Repeat this next line out loud:
I am Black, I am beautiful, and I am worth it.

Self-Worth

Self-worth is simply the sense of a value that a person has for themselves. This word is commonly interchanged with self-confidence, self-respect, and self-esteem. I personally believe that all these terms have different meanings. While they all refer to how someone feels about themselves, they differ in many ways. I challenge you to simply look at self-worth as the value that you place upon your life.

Many of us place value on ourselves by comparing ourselves to others. Comparing ourselves to others is one of the key components that stands in the way of feeling self-worthy. The act of comparing ourselves to others causes us to devalue ourselves and we began to walk as if we don't matter or feel like we will never be enough.

Self- worth is a foreign concept to most of us. We are fed things in our lives via advertisements, the educational system, as well as our family that serve as a marker for our worth. In advertising, we must be or wear a specified brand or look a certain way to be worthy of achievement. For example, the brand Nike makes us feel like if we wear their shoes, we will be great at sports. Education, our worth is graded based on academic achievement rather than knowledge gained. And do not get me started on the inequality of the educations that we receive; I'll save that for another book. In many family systems, the "good child" is the one who obeys specific orders or does a great job at the chores or just remains quiet.

In the world of social media, our worth is determined by the amount of subscribers and likes we have. Worth is not determined by content. I am extremely surprised at the affect that social media has on our young Black girls. Doing it for the 'gram or participating in challenges appear to be more important than self-confidence.

For this next exercise, let's examine your self-worth.

Do this exercise when you start your day. Tell yourself why you are worthy of love. I have provided 15 positive affirmations simply as a road map. You are the driver of your destiny; therefore, you choose how to begin each day. Why not choose to begin it by loving you? Yes, you woke up like this!

I am worthy of love because:

I am unstoppable.	I am driven.
I am excited to meet my goals.	I am strong.
I am motivated.	I am committed.
I am ready for growth.	I accept the challenge of change.
I am love.	I have a purpose.
I am who God created me to be.	I am built for success.
I am heading in the right direction.	I am able to trust me.
I believe in myself.	I am passionate.

I am unapologetically me.

Got more? Write them down!

_____

_____

_____

_____

Lately, vision boards have become all the rave. A vision board is a visual way to set goals for yourself. It is done so using pictures, words, and a little bit of creativity. Vision boards are amazing; however, during this journey to self-love, I would like you to create an affirmation board.

Self-Worth Exercise: Affirmation Board

Create an Affirmation Board: Using pictures, quotes, and creativity, create a visual of the positive affirmations from the activity above. It doesn't matter if you aren't artistic, have fun with the project. Then hang it in a place that you can see it. Each time you walk past it, you will be given a visual of the wonderful person that you are.

Self-Esteem

Self-esteem is how we think or feel about ourselves. Self-esteem is liking ourselves. It is my belief that self-esteem is a biproduct of knowing your value.

Self-Confidence

Self-confidence is not an evaluation of self. Self-confidence is reflective of a person's drive. This is typically reflective of a specific activity or area.

Self-Esteem/Self-Confidence Exercise
A love Letter to Self

For our next exercise, we will be writing ourselves a love letter. Why? My response is, why not? Writing a love letter to yourself will help you examine some of the good that you see within yourself. An additional challenge for this exercise is to exclude all buts. Love you out loud, or at least on paper.

Dear Me,

_____
_____
_____
_____
_____
_____
_____
_____
_____
_____
_____
_____
_____
_____
_____
_____
_____

Chapter 4: Be Kind to Yourself

I end each of my clinical sessions by saying the phrase, "Be kind to yourself." I know it may sound slightly corny, but we often need to know that it is okay to be good to ourselves. We use so much of our energy pouring into others that by the time we get to our glasses, the substance is gone.

Being kind to yourself does not mean be lazy, or not do what you set out to do. Simply put, it means allowing yourself to enjoy your journey through life. It is my belief that we all require just a little grace to battle this thing called life.

While I do believe in divine grace, this is not the grace that I am referring to. But since we are here, let's explore divine grace. Divine grace is a theological term which refers to the divine grace that is given to us through God's love. This grace comes without IOU's and doesn't get taken back when things go the wrong way. His grace is ours because He wants us to have it and it is ever so necessary.

Within the Christian faith there is a rule which asks Christians to love thy neighbor as thy self. Loosely translated this means to love your neighbor just as much as you love you. I think this gives us the allowance to first love ourselves.

I've given the assignment to be kind to themselves to thousands of clients throughout my career and they have all asked the same question—*How?* The mother believes that being kind to herself will take away some of her strength from her children. The executive in some way feels that being kind to self will take away their edge. This is not the case. Being kind to yourself will only add to you. Imagine having a mother who loves herself. Wouldn't you think that her children will see this love and learn that they too should love themselves?

Imagine that executive who took lunch breaks, exudes positive energy, and has a bright outlook. Wouldn't you think that this self-care would reflect on her staff?

We pride ourselves on being good mother, good wives, workers, and the list goes on and on. How many of us pride ourselves on being a good us? I want everyone to see the value of who they are in the present moment. If there is one thing that I know for certain is that tomorrow is not promised and yesterday is never coming back. Loving ourselves in the present moment is all we truly have.

Self-care

Self-care consists of those things that we do to evoke positive feelings within ourselves. Some of us work out, while others go to the spa. Self-care is key to showing love to ourselves because it allows us to feel positive in the moment. I believe strongly in paying yourself first. This does not mean using the mortgage for a spa day, but it does mean creating an avenue to enjoy and relax.

Self- Care Exercise:

Do something, anything that only benefits you. Washing the laundry does not count neither does housework. Do something that brings you happiness without causing guilt.

What did you do?

_____
_____
_____
_____
_____

How did doing this make you feel?

_____
_____
_____
_____

As a child, my mother would frequently take long baths. She'd get her Jean Nate and Calgon, draw her a nice warm bath, and disappear for what felt like hours. I remember her saying, "Don't knock on this door unless someone is bleeding or there is a fire." As a child I did not understand what she was doing. She was Momma and Momma needed to be available 24/7. I remember thinking to myself, "What if I need an emergency sandwich, or my sister looked at me too long and I needed a referee?"

We all, for the most part, respected her wishes. She'd bathe for a million hours but when she opened the door she appeared to be super mom. I think her baths were her self-care. We grew up in a family system where we did not have money to "waste" on salons, spas, or girls trips, but mom found her way to have self-care moments.

As Black and brown women we carry guilt everywhere we go. I'm not sure why. Maybe it's the weight of the family on our shoulders, or the guilt associated with needing to prove ourselves to everyone. I believe that this guilt is the very thing that holds us back.

Have you ever heard the early 2000's song "Bag Lady" by Erykah Badu? If not, stop reading and YouTube it. I recall my first time hearing it. I'll never forget it. I was a senior in college. During my college years I visited my mother weekly. She and I were running errands and the song came on the Chicago-based radio station, WGCI 107.5 FM. First, I was grooving then, I started listening to the words. I literally started crying uncontrollably. My mother thought I'd lost my entire mind. The song to me represents the literal and emotional baggage that we as women carry throughout our lives. Some believe that it is reflective of male-female relationships, but I personally applied it to my life, not just some dude.

Within the song she sang:

"Bag lady, you gone hurt yo' back carrying all them bags like that. I bet nobody ever told you all you must hold onto is you."

I promise I just got chills writing that one line. We spend our lives carrying bags that are ours, were ours earlier in life, or heck, some of us are carrying bags that do not even belong to us. Aren't those bags so very heavy? What if you put the bags down just for a moment and love you in the here and now?

Put down those past bags – Self-Forgiveness

Our minds are very powerful things. Self-forgiveness sounds so daunting doesn't it? What does self-forgiveness entail? Our past experiences should help to teach us. They should help us to learn and grow beyond or because of the many experiences that we have had. But for many of us they are the very things that prevent our growth. We get caught in that moment and until we forgive ourselves, we are trapped in the web of past hurts. People say just let it go, but that is easier said than done, right?

One of my Michaeisms is, "Recycle your cans, not your can'ts." Those past tense bags that we are carrying often prevent us from growing. If you are constantly beating yourself up for having failed in the past how can you prepare for the next endeavor?

An example that prevents growth is failed relationships. Many of us bring the pain of previous relationships into every experience of our lives. Yep, every experience. Relationships are any connections that individuals have with other people, not necessarily dating or marriage. Relationships can be connections with family, parents, friends, teachers, a mentor, a teacher, anyone. We have the tendency to carry all that pain with us. I would love for you to take this time to visualize yourself taking the life lessons out of those negative relationships and throwing the rest of that garbage in the garbage. Yes, the garbage! Your man cheated—garbage! Mother called you names—garbage! Lied to—garbage! You get the point. Now look at what you learned. Now let's look at what we keep from these situations. Your man cheated you learned your worth- keep. Your mother called you names you learned to love yourself- keep. People lied to you learned the value of being trustworthy -keep. You were able to love—keep! You learned life lessons—

Keep! You grew—keep! After your visualization, take the time to write out what you threw away versus what you kept. You may need to refer to this in the future.

Let it Go Exercise

Garbage:
_____
_____
_____
_____

Recycle:
_____
_____
_____
_____

Instead of trashing the pain we tend to compartmentalize it. That means we put it in little folders in our brains and pull them out when *necessary*. Have your ever said, "I don't mess with women; they are too messy"? Or perhaps, "Men aren't crap"? (Yes, that's a very nice way of saying it.) We build these walls to prevent hurt; we build these walls to prevent the good, bad, or ugly from having a chance to hurt us.

It is okay to allow yourself to heal. Forgive that young woman who was hurt by her boyfriend or husband. Forgive that woman who was hurt by not getting a raise. Forgive that woman who messed up so many times she can't count. If you do then maybe you will let your guard down enough to grow because of these experiences instead of allowing them to keep you stagnant.

Back to the "Bag Lady" analogy. The song goes on to say, *"If you start breathing things will get better,"* which is my point exactly.

How do I forgive myself?

Self-forgiveness simply starts with acknowledging wrongdoings. After you acknowledge the wrongdoing, show yourself that you are wonderful despite the things you did. Show growth and learn from the wrongdoing. From all our mistakes, trials and hiccups comes the opportunity to learn, grow and mature.

Need an example? You stayed in a relationship too long. This man was no good for you, but you stayed because you vowed for better or worse, or even worse. You stayed and you know why; we won't waste time rationalizing why. You learned that you deserve better, and within your next relationship you set boundaries which include what you will and will not take. Forgive yourself for not "doing what you ought to." Learn from the situation and simply put, do what you need to. Show the next person or the current person that you are better than such treatment.

Sometimes self-forgiveness is not so easy. What if the negative experience was a trauma? What if you had no real involvement in the matter? What if it was rape, molestation, domestic violence (DV) or any other trauma? Find a great therapist and allow yourself to work through your feelings and emotions. Forgive yourself so you can live. These hurts require self-forgiveness because even though these situations were not our fault, we tend to blame ourselves. You know what I mean. *Maybe I should've done 'x'; why didn't I 'z'?* It's time to let go of those nagging thoughts. Forgive you because you deserve to live. Allow the 5-year-old girl in you to heal so that the 30-year-old can live.

Next the song also says, *"You can't hurry up cuz you got too much stuff."* I take this to mean that once you get to the place where you are ready to fly, all the negative experiences prevent you from spreading your wings to grow. The end of the song literally calls us all out and pleads for us to let our bags go.

The song goes on to say, *"One day all them bags gone get in your way."* In my opinion, this statement means that we spend so much time in the negative space in life that when our blessings come along, we miss them. We can't be in a peaceful or happy space because all the garbage is trashing our existence.

The song breaks down "bad ladies" into different categories: Garbage bag, grocery bag lady, Gucci bag lady, paper sack lady, nickel bag lady and the backpack lady. Let's take a gander at all these categories, shall we?

The Garbage Bag Lady

I think the garbage bag lady refer to those of us who are carrying around literal booboo, fecal matter, crap. All the negative words that people have said is garbage. We carry those things as though they are our heartbeats. I need you to look at these things as exactly what they are, crap. Instead of them being your heartbeat, they are literally the plaque that is clogging your arteries preventing health.

The Grocery Bag Lady

While I can relate with all the ladies identified in this song's lyrics, I identify most with the grocery bag lady. This is the woman who sacrifices her world for her family. She must rationalize doing even the smallest things for herself. She works her fingers to the bone and in return wants nothing but to see her family members smile.

Many grocery bag ladies work 40 plus hours a week and then work another 100 hours. Her hard work often goes unnoticed.

Story Time: Wanna hear it? Here it Go!
I have a wonderful friend. Heck, friend is the wrong word; she's my sister. My friend has four children of all age ranges. She is the pure essence of what a mother is

supposed to be. She had two of her children at a very young age. Wanting the best for her children, she took both to college with her. Yes, you read correctly. Her and her two boys went to a university together. She earned her undergraduate degree, but she didn't stop there. She took both of her children with her as she received her master's degree.

She had two additional children, two amazing young women. She went on to receive yet another master's degree.

One of my nieces wished to gain a career in acting. My sister was at the top of her career pulling in well over six figures. She stopped what she was doing, packed up and moved to California to help her daughter reach her dreams. While helping her daughter reach her goals, she was diagnosed with breast cancer. Yes, breast cancer. My sister attended chemotherapy, radiation and pursued a doctoral degree all while driving my niece to auditions.

My sister's story doesn't end there. Somewhere between her move from the Midwest to California, her youngest daughter was diagnosed with autism. She went into action mode. She gathered all her resources and got her child connected to services to assure that she had all she needed. All while fighting breast cancer.

Yes, you guessed it, my sister's story does not end there. She founded a non-profit organization to assist survivors of breast cancer. She wrote a book to promote the healing of other women. She shows the overall strength of the "grocery bag lady." Instead of focusing her efforts on herself, she focused all this energy into assuring that her children were well developed, and able to live their dreams.

The Gucci Bag Lady

I think the Gucci bag ladies are those of us who are either affluent or pretending to be affluent. These women are trying to have "what they are having," living as though they need to live up to some standard created by someone else, rich or not. Honestly, once the Gucci leaves the store it has zero value. So, you've literally spent your life carrying around the Gucci bag that is literally worthless. What you have, earn or wear does not define you; you define you.

The Paper Sack Lady

I believe the paper sack ladies are the women who are struggling. Women who may not be wealthy but are attempting to care for themselves in a world that may not respect them. These are the women who are experiencing socio-economic issues as related to poverty, or lack of resources. I include the lack of resources in this category because simply having financial resources, does not equate overall success or happiness. Lacking guidance and direction can lead a person to a place where they feel empty or hopeless. I challenge all my *"paper sack ladies,"* to stop using the phrase, "I'm broke." You are not broken, you "temporarily lack the financial means." Saying that you are "broke" makes you feel broken.

The Nickel Bag Lady

I believe that the Nickel Bag ladies are struggling with addiction. Sometimes we use things such as drugs, alcohol, shopping, sex, or love to mask our pain. This is called self-medicating. The addicted woman is not only numb to life but is also numb to creating solutions.

The Backpack Lady

The backpack lady is the lady who tries to show herself to the world educationally. I spoke about her earlier in that Black women are the most educated group in the United States. She shoots for the stars while attaining the education that she deems is necessary to make her mark on the world.

The next words of the song that are striking to me are: *"So, pack light."* Forgive yourself so you can make the next steps towards loving yourself. I don't know which woman you identify with. I personally identify with them all.
"I bet you love can make it better."
These words are representative of the self-forgiveness and self-love that we must gain to achieve true happiness.

While many of us fall into a combination of many of these ladies, I hope that we allow ourselves the freedom to "pack light." Forgive you so you can walk in your truth. The next chapter seeks to help you forgive others in efforts to become the best version of yourself.

While journeying through life it is important to develop coping strategies to assist you in dealing with issues that you may experience.

Coping Assessment Exercise:

What tools do you currently have to cope with life's stressors?
1. Identify the problem. Just one problem.
2. How is the problem making you feel?
3. Identify the tools you already have in your toolbox to address the issue?
4. Apply the tool.
5. Self-evaluate. How are you feeling after using the tool(s)?
6. Apply more tools.

This tool should be applied to any stressor.

Chapter 5: Protect Yourself

People often overstep your boundaries because you haven't given them boundaries in the first place. Think about times when you've practiced your *no's*. You've said *no*, you meant *no*, and you did just the opposite.

That's an example of you not setting boundaries. When I call my nephew for a chat and he is "busy" (whatever busy is for a 4-year-old), he politely says, "Sorry TiTi, I'm playing the game and I'll call you back maybe Tuesday." Guess what I do? Yes, you've guessed it! I wait for his call back and I know maybe it will be coming on Tuesday. So, if a 4-year-old can set boundaries so can you.

Setting Boundaries Exercise

Before saying yes because the people pleaser in you wants to make others happy, ask yourself a few questions.

Am I doing this because I want to or because I feel that I have to?
Will my actions assist the person I'm helping?
Will my actions enable the person that I'm helping?
Will doing this action bring me joy?
Will doing this action cause me pain?
Will doing this action cost me money?
Will there be an equal amount of cash or in-kind activities done by all parties?
Am I emotionally available to do this action?
Will participating in this action cause me to feel resentment?

Please remember that the word *no* is a complete sentence. *No.* This means that after you have said the word there is no comma, semi colon, or colon. It is simply *no*. You do not owe anyone any explanations.

I do understand that there is some guilt associated with saying *no*, however, if you don't protect yourself, who will? I'm not saying that friends and family are aiming to take advantage of you. I am saying that on some occasions they automatically assume that you are fine with doing an action because you never say *no*. If saying *no* is too hard, add thank you to the end of it. *No, thank you.*

Okay, so we all aren't as good at setting boundaries as my nephew. So, lets discuss ways in which to set boundaries:

1. ***Decide what your limits are.*** If you don't know your limits you cannot be angry that people push you past them. Deciding your limits are important because it serves a guide not only for others but also for yourself.

Financial Limits

If the task or person requires money. Set a specific dollar amount and only give that amount or less. I'm not saying to be selfish, but I am saying give what you can afford to give. Both emotionally and financially. If giving more that you can give will put a financial strain on you, give what you can afford to. If giving will put an emotional strain on you, i.e., you feel used or undervalued, give what you can emotionally afford to give.

Emotional Limits

Providing support also requires emotional support. While financial strain may be easier to notice, emotional strain often requires more from a person. Try going into situations or relationships with emotional limits having already been decided. Being an emotional support for others requires you to be able to process the emotional needs of others while trying to protect yourself also. If possible, when taking an emotional call or having the emotional cup of coffee with a friend, try to schedule these at times where you are in a healthy space emotionally.

2. ***Understand your feelings.***

Understanding where you are emotionally on a subject matter not only helps you, but it also helps the person that you are trying to support. Ask yourself how you feel about a subject matter then set your boundaries based upon your needs also.

3. ***Understand why you need boundaries.***

We all need boundaries. Having boundaries is necessary because it allows you to know how much of yourself to give to a situation. As a therapist I was taught by my professors to never give more of myself to a client's situation than they are willing to give.

Story Time: Wanna hear it? Here it Go!

A wife has a husband who is struggling with addiction. She can recognize her husband's triggers and almost time his episodes to a science. Whenever she notices the triggers, she jumps into survival mode. She tries to make the house as quiet as possible; she cooks all her husband's favorite meals, and she makes sure everything is perfect. However, the episode happens no matter how much effort she puts into preventing them. Why? The answer is quite easy. The episodes occur because he allows them.

Enabling

An enabler is a person whose actions or inactions allow a person to continue in self-destructive behaviors. Enabling is typically seen in a negative light, however, most enablers are not doing so deliberately.

According to the American Psychological Association, enabling occurs not only within relationships stricken with addictions but also within relationships whereby individuals maintain any harmful behavior. Enabling does not mean that you support the behavior. It means that your behaviors do not help the situation. As a part of a relationship, I encourage you to try empowerment.

Empowerment

Empowerment means that you offer ways to get to the solution to the problem. As a support system, give tools, resources or teach them skills. Remember the saying: "Give a man a fish and he eats for one night. Teach a man to fish he will eat for a lifetime." That's empowerment. I am sure that many of us have given our loved ones plenty of fish. But how many of us have given a fishing lesson?

4. *Be direct in your responses to others.*

Being direct in your responses to others is not being mean. It is the exact opposite. By being direct, your loved one clearly understands what and how you will assist them.

5. *Never apologize for having boundaries.*

So, you have decided to provide to a friend or family member, please do not apologize for what you are able to give. Remember as a part of your loved ones support system, you are choosing to empower them not to enable them. Apologizing for your abilities only allows guilt to creep in. Then what happens? Yes, you guessed it! You do more than you were emotionally or financially able to give. And the cycle of resentment begins.

6. *Trust your intuition.*

Our guts usually don't lie. If your gut tells you something, please believe it. If this means proceed with caution, please do so. Other times it means run. In that case, run. Eventually, what our gut was trying to tell us will come out. Be patient and trust yourself.

7. *Take care of yourself within all your relationships.*

Within relationships we expect our person or people to take care of us. No one else knows how to take care of us like we do. We cannot expect others to protect us against them.

8. *Reevaluate boundaries to see if they are working for you.*

Sometimes we set boundaries and they aren't quite working well for us. Please remember it is okay to go back and reevaluate your boundaries. You are allowed to change your mind. You can set stricter ones once you have gotten to know a situation. You can also loosen boundaries (just a tad) if you find yourself wanting to do more. Loosening boundaries are based on your personal desires to do more, not the other person's request for more.

Boundaries are not brick walls. Boundaries are a set of standards that you set for the way that you would like to be treated.

Setting Boundaries with Self Healthy Living

Another area of self-care is healthy living. No, I'm not saying lose a bunch of weight or go on some fad diet. My challenge is to treat your body in a way that shows that you love you.

Many of us avoid doctors' appointments for various reasons. Finances, time, or simply not wanting to know what is going on. I am guilty of this myself. Before I had those two strokes, my body gave me warnings. I heard them and ignored them. I made excuses: *I'll go later. I can't afford another doctor's bill.* My excuses went on and on until I was forced to take care of myself. Please don't be like Michae'; she was wrong, and she messed up. I forgive me now and am striving for a healthier life.

Car Exercise

If you could have any luxury car on the planet (free of charge) what would it be?
_____
_____
_____
_____
_____
_____

What kind of gas does it take?
_____
_____
_____
_____
_____
_____

Would you get regularly scheduled maintenance?
_____
_____
_____

Would you clean it inside and out?
_____
_____
_____
_____
_____

Would you let just any one drive it?
_____
_____
_____
_____
_____

What would you do if the check engine light came on?
_____
_____
_____
_____
_____

Now replace the luxury car with you.

What kind of person do you want to be?
_____
_____
_____
_____
_____

What kind of fuel works best to keep you in fine condition?
___

When was your last doctor's visit?
___

Do you keep yourself in your best shape?
___

How many people are being allowed to drive your motivation, actions, and movements?
___

Many of us are running through life with our check engine light on, on an empty tank, dented and bruised. YOU are in control of your destiny. Try self-care, it's a great place to show you that you are worthy. Stop treating your luxury self like a humpty.

The next chapter is geared towards cleaning house in hopes of getting you to a place of peace, love, and self-love.

Chapter 6: Cleaning House

Imagine your life like a theater. This is your life thus you are the star of the show. Visualize yourself standing center stage all decked out, Diana Rossesque, preparing to put on your best performance yet. Isn't this a wonderful feeling? It is exciting, liberating, and frightening at the same time. But you've made it and you've got this. Now peek out stage left; the house is packed. It's your turn and all eyes are on you.

In your typical theater, there are several seating options. There is the orchestra or VIP seating, the good seats, the okay seats, and the balcony. Because we practice social distancing in our theater, we have no room for standing room only options. Then there is the parking lot.

Many of us have people in our front row seating who belong in the balcony. Some of us feel that just because someone has a specified title in our lives that we should automatically provide them with VIP seating. Why? I'm not saying that these people don't belong in your world but why VIP? Perhaps you just need to reassign seating. You may have people in the balcony who deserve good seats. Remember this is your life and you have the power to place people in the areas of your life based on who they are, not who you'd like them to be.

What happens if you are all queued up and the people you've chosen to open your curtain fails to do so? Your show can't begin. Maybe we have toxic relatives or friends, but simply because they have the title of an aunt, cousin, brother, sister, mother, father, or friend we automatically give them stagehand duties. This could be for several reasons. One reason could be because the person simply lacked the skills to do the duty in your life that you've assigned to them. You may question how someone could not have the skill to open a curtain. Maybe they are in the middle of their storm and can't perform the duty as assigned. No, this doesn't mean that you automatically dismiss them from the show. This means that you give them a duty in your life that they can perform. Another reason for them being unable to perform their duty could be because they have other skills that could be used elsewhere in the show. The final reason that I'll provide for this show disaster is that the person given the duty is not invested in your show. Instead of inviting them to the good seats or balcony, it may be best that they no longer are invited to the show. This may sound cruel, however, if they have no investment, why waste the seat?

Sticks and Stones

Remember the childhood saying, "Sticks and stones may break my bones, but words will never hurt me?" As an adult I simply wish that saying were true. While words don't cause immediate physical pain, they have the tendency to cause long-term emotional pain. As humans we may say that words don't hurt but we pick up those words and allow ourselves to build walls for protection and rejection. We build walls around our hearts to protect ourselves from being hurt again. However, those very walls that we have built may prevent others who belong there from getting in.

Sticks and Stones Exercise

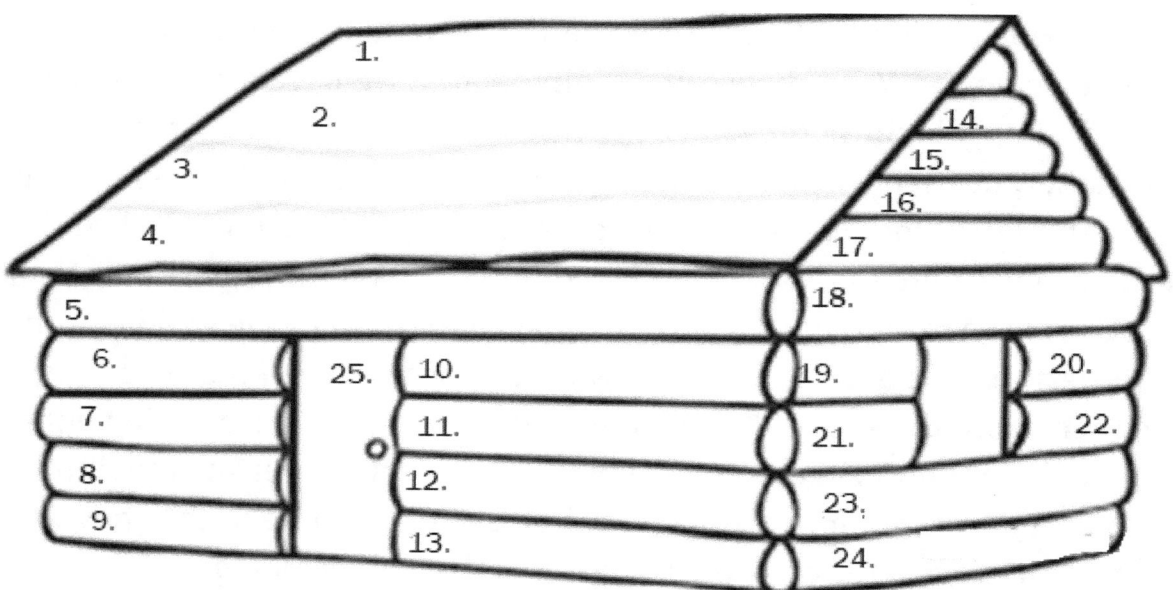

Recall the story of the 3 pigs. Houses made of sticks aren't so strong, so let's tear those down. Using the stones, explain to yourself why you are willing to let go of the hurtful words, negative self-talk and overall painful words that have prevented your growth. This exercise is visual. Maybe if you can see the words and know the truth, you can begin to be your truth and not the negative words. In each of the sections of the house of sticks, list the negative things that people have said to you that you still carry around today.

These are the stones that you are using to shatter the negative connections that you have made between yourself and these words. Next to the stones write out your reasons for letting go of these hurtful words.

Of course, we learn from our past. Instead of building walls with negatives, we need to process our feelings thus creating changes that help us to see the life lessons in things instead of rejecting what life has to offer.

Journaling

Many of us view journaling as something else to do, like a task. While others avoid it because it can be painful. What if you change your thinking on what journaling is? Think of your journal as your best friend. You talk to your bestie about everything right? The good, bad, or totally jacked up things, right?

Get a special journal just for you. Make it reflective of who you are; it doesn't have to be expensive, just structured. Do not use it for your bills, grocery list or math class, please and thank you. This is the place for your feelings, emotions, dreams, and solutions.

Follow this simple 3-step process to begin:
1. Start with something positive.
2. Write the stuff you need to say.
3. Tie up the loose ends.

Starting your journal entry on a positive note is to remind yourself that even in your painful moments, there are little rays of hope. Writing what you need to say is a way to process your thoughts and feelings. Finally, ending by reminding yourself of what your steps are for working on the issues at hand provides you hope for the future.

The goal of journaling is to allow you to process your own feelings or emotions. Journaling should cleanse you. Don't worry if the sentences don't sound right. Don't worry about your handwriting. Don't worry if it does not sound like William Shakespeare's greatest work. That's not the point. Writing pen to paper helps you process your feelings and take them out of your head and heart and place them on paper. Like a detox so to speak. If all you write is one word and it feels better than when you started, you've completed your goal.

There was this show that aired when I was a child called *Doogie Houser, M.D.* where this teen doctor wrote in his journal at the end of each show detailing the struggles and the lessons learned from his day. Please don't expect your journal entries to be like Dr. Howsers! You will not fix all your issues within a 30-minute period. Just starting the process is sufficient. Processing your feelings is the first step.

Journaling Exercise:

Sample Journal set up:

Date:_____

The Good Word: *(In this section challenge yourself by saying one good thing. Remember your journal is yours, no one other than you must understand your good words. Example: The sun is shining in Chicago today.)*

The Stuff: *(This is what you need to say. Write your feelings, emotions, thoughts. Say what's on your mind and in your heart. Example: I had a very challenging day at my new job. I felt like I just wasn't doing anything correctly.)*

Goal Towards Fixing the Stuff: *(This is what you are doing about it. Remind yourself that the conflict is not forever. Give yourself action items to make changes in the future. Example: Yes, my day was challenging. I will schedule a meeting with my supervisor for clarity surrounding projects.)*

Chapter 7: Celebrating Even the Small Wins

The journey to self-love comes with its share of ups and downs. Thus, it is important to remember to celebrate ones wins. Celebrating your wins helps to promote growth. These small celebrations provide us with the energy necessary to propel forward when we hit the harder parts in our journeys.

Story Time: Wanna hear it? Here it go!
At age 23, Jazmine set out on a journey to become a dentist. Jazmine had several circumstances to overcome. She was a single mother, lacked financial means and was the first in her family to attend college. She began her journey by completing a certification program to become a dental hygienist. For Jazmine, becoming a dental hygienist allowed her to have the financial means to achieve her goal. After graduating from the certificate program, she celebrated. The celebratory moment came with the purchase of a new pair of shoes. With money in hand, Jazmine then enrolled in a junior college. During her time at junior college, Jazmine took her basic biology and chemistry courses. After the completion of each course, she had a small celebration with her best friends and cheerleaders. Jazmine went on to receive an associate degree in biology. And she celebrated it. Jazmine was accepted into the university. She celebrated the acceptance into the program. She celebrated throughout the program. She earned a bachelor's in biology and yes, she celebrated. Jazmine then applied to dental school. And of course, there was a celebration. Jazmine is now a dentist and owns her own practice. In Jazmine's story one can see the benefits of celebrating yourself. Celebrating yourselves gives us the motivation to continue to move forward and strive for a personal best.

According to BJ Fogg, celebrating one's wins makes an imprint on our brain that essentially helps with motivation and change. According to Fogg, big change starts by making tiny changes. Behavior change starts by making tiny habits that ultimately help one in reaching larger goals (Fogg, 2019).

Celebrating wins doesn't necessarily mean having a large event or spending a great deal of money. Celebrating a win could simply be telling yourself that you are amazing, telling yourself that you rocked after completing a task, or going to get a scoop of ice cream (unless your new habit is fitness related). Take a few moments to write out a few ways that you can celebrate you.

Celebrating Your Wins Exercise

After accomplishing a win, I can:

1._____

2._____

3._____

4._____

5._____

6._____

7._____

8._____

9._____

10._____

Fogg discusses the tiny change model for change. This model states that change occurs when three things are present to facilitate change:

1. **Motivation (a rational for your change)**
   Motivation is a purpose for actions, readiness, and objectives. It is important to identify what motivates you because it provides you with the rational for change. Simply stating that I want to be a better parent is great however, stating that I wish to be a better parent for my 3-year-old daughter gives depth to the goal.

2. **Ability (Physical, mental, and emotional capacity)**
   Having the motivation for change is great however, motivation without ability sounds more like a dream to me. The ability to make change touches upon physical, financial, environmental, or mental health restrictions that may prevent change. For example, the mother who is motivated to be a better parent for her 3-year-old child may set a goal of attending a parenting class with 10 sessions. Lack of funding may prevent reaching this goal. Should the mother cancel the goal or change the tiny thing? Until resources become available, this mother may choose to add reading a book to her child before bed. The action of reading the book is a change that is attainable and will aid to her goal of becoming a better parent. After mastering this tiny habit, the mother can revisit this goal and set additional tiny habits.

3. **Call to action or trigger (Things that you already do in normal life)**
A call to action or triggers are actions that use to trigger change. These triggers are things that we naturally do in our lives. For example, bedtime is the call to action in the previous example.

Look at your life. Identify tiny behaviors that you would like to change in your life. Identify tiny behaviors that you can incorporate in your life and make the change. Most of us tend to design goals for a specific outcome. For example, we change eating habits to lose weight. This model stresses the importance of creating behaviors that lead to our desired outcome.

Story Time: Wanna hear it? Here it Go!

This is the story of Clarise. She grew up as the middle child. As a child she often felt left out, and under acknowledged. Because of those feelings she made the conscious choice to use her life to uplift the lives of others. She had no clue as to how to make this happen, however she did not let this stop her mission. She began by educating herself and enclosing herself in her community. She volunteered at soup kitchens, substance abuse treatment centers and community growth events. Clarise used every fiber in her being to help uplift every person that she encountered. She celebrated even the smallest of her client's victories.

Today, she founded a non-profit organization, wrote books, and continues her life's journey of positively impacting the lives of as many people as possible. In reading Claris's story, one can see that setting even the largest of goals can be met by simply making the first step.

Goal Setting Exercise: Mind Map

Complete the mind map below by identifying a goal that you wish to achieve. Identify what motivates you to reach this goal. Can you reach this goal? What small things can you do to reach this goal? Then celebrate each small thing as you complete it.

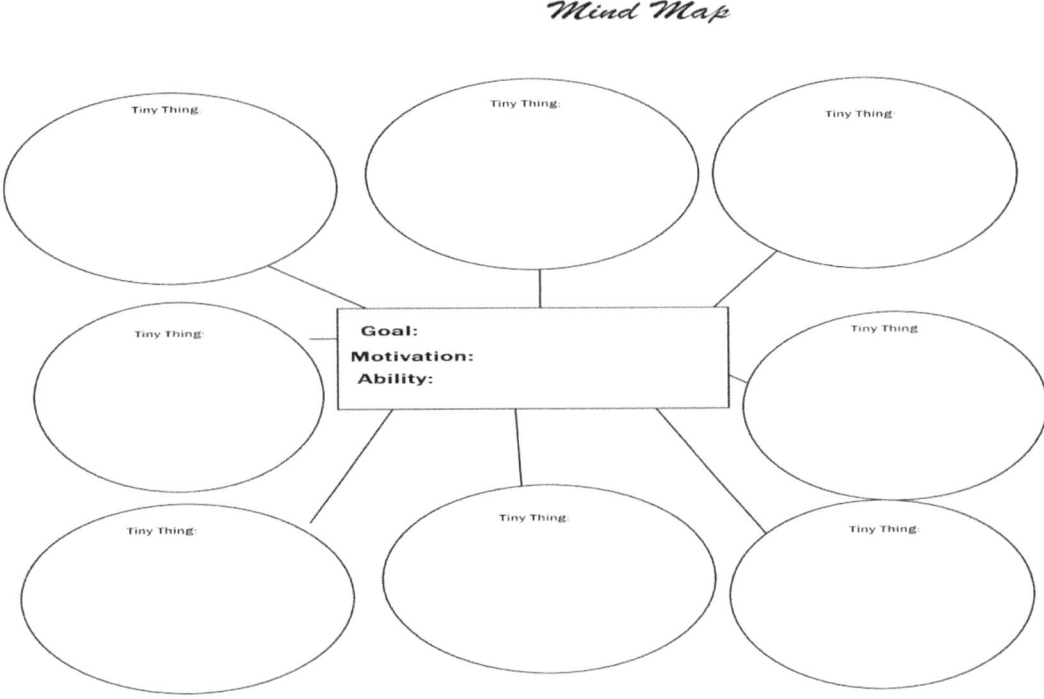

When applying this to your real life, remember that each step is important however, the celebration is key to continued success. It is important to remember to practice changing our own behaviors. Change will not occur over night; however, practicing helps change to become permanent.

Chapter 8: Dating and Loving You

This may appear to be an odd chapter to add to a self-help workbook however, I thought it to be a valuable topic to broach during the self-love journey. Many of us see our value through the relationships that we have with others. For example, we see ourselves in terms of what others think of us.

For this chapter, I'd like for you to focus on the relationships that you have with or are striving for with the person who you are dating, were dating, married to or the relationships that have caused trauma or angst in your perception of yourself. Or maybe even the one that got away.

Throughout our history of the United States of America, Black love has been difficult to say the very least. During the years of slavery Black marriage was forbidden, therefore Black marriages were not legally recognized. Our connections with the opposite sex were only viewed in ways of economic growth for the slave master. Ultimately, Black women were paired with "bucks" who were Black men that the master believed would produce strong, healthy children who were born slaves. Black women were raped while Black men were bound and unable to serve as a support for the Black woman. Black children were sold away from their mothers, husbands from their wives, and wives from their husbands.

During reconstruction, violence split up the Black family. Later, poverty played a role in the dissolution of the Black family. The welfare system mandated that Black women remained single to gain any governmental support. The rise of incarceration and inherited poverty was yet another culprit which disrupted Black love.

Currently 70% of all Black women in America will never be married due to no fault of their own. In Dianne M. Stewart's book *Black Women, Black Love*, she attributes this statistic to three major factors: inherited poverty, the idealization of the patriotic nuclear family and Eurocentric standards of beauty. It's a very interesting read.

I will spare you the rest of the history lesson. Of those things that I just said, I'd like you to look closely at this sentence: *Currently 70% of all Black women in America will never be married **due to no fault of their own**.* No fault of their own. Yes, I had to say it a third time just in case you needed to read that.

It's not your fault. I believe that we should own what is ours. What you may be guilty of is not loving yourself enough during your relationships, losing yourself in your relationships, or holding onto relationships that are not healthy for you just to have someone.

Every frog you kiss will not become prince charming. In fact, no frog you kiss will become prince charming. A frog and or toad is going to remain that, a frog. You cannot love the miserable out of a person. Do you know what I mean by that? This means that no matter how much you invest in someone else, they will not change unless they decide to change. This fact is a very difficult one to swallow, isn't it? You can cook dinners, fix a man's credit, or clean the kitchen better, and think this is the magic potion to evolve the frog. If anything, it simply helps them to stay in your lily pad and become your dependent. So, ask yourself, do I want a dependent or do I want a healthy relationship?

Many of us do not have examples of what a healthy relationship is due to the reasons stated above. However, we can learn from the negative relationships what we do not want. I have complied some of the components of a negative relationship.

Why do we stay in unhealthy relationships?

According to the University of Southern California, people enter and stay in unhealthy relationships for a host of reasons including but not limited to, desire for companionship, lack of financial stability, or lack of knowledge of what a healthy relationship is. According to the USC, remaining in an unhealthy relationship is frequently tied to a psychological method called idealization.

Idealization is an unconscious or semiconscious wish that has been developed by cultural and biological factors. These factors ultimately blind people from seeing the truth. These factors prevent us from seeing the red flags that the other has shown us within the relationship. While these factors may be clear to those around us, those involved are blinded.

Relationships add to you. They are not supposed to drain you or strip you.

Ice Cream Exercise:
What is your favorite ice cream?

You represent that ice cream. For the example's sake, we will go with strawberries and cream (my favorite). Now what happens if Johnny comes along and demands your strawberries? Or you get involved with Johnny and think you are supposed to give him your strawberries. As time progresses he will begin to request the cream, sugar, milk, heck everything thus leaving you with ice. A cold brick of ice. You've lost your flavor, your zest, your you.

A relationship should be more like an ice cream sundae. It should add to you. I like gummy bears in my sundaes. So, the relationship communication can be the gummy bears, fun can be the nuts, learning can be the whipped cream and honesty can be the cherry on the top. At the core there is still the strawberry ice cream. If all those things are removed you can still stand alone. Our relationships do not define us, we define the relationships. Standing on your own two feet does not make you undesirable; it makes you more desirable, not so much for him, her, or them but for you.

Domestic Violence

This is a subject that is so hard for me. As a domestic violence survivor, I've felt all the excuses that one tells themselves. If I would have cleaned better, he would not have hit me. If I'd been better in bed or if I'd been a better woman, he would not have put his hands on me. For me, the *if I's* became so plentiful that I can't even fathom writing them all.

He's the frog. Not you. Get help! Not for him but for you. Save this number in your phone under a name your abuser will never think of. I personally used Nancy. **(800)799-7233**. Pack a bag and put it at a relative's house and when you are ready to leave, you do not have to waste your time trying to figure things out. Your healthy mind already did it for you.

Tell someone what you are going through. Do not get beaten verbally or physically in silence. Yes, you may hear things like, "You are crazy for staying," or "You are exaggerating." Without calling anyone out, a family member told me that, and I quote, "He only beats you because you let him, then you call your family and get everyone involved in your mess." Don't risk your life waiting for the change. Violence is violence. Being a survivor of domestic violence does not mean that you are weak.

Chapter 9: Treat Yourself Like Someone You Love

This chapter unites all the components of the previous chapters in efforts to assure that you can continue your journey to self-love.

Remember self-love is giving yourself permission to love the you that you are. Self-love is not selfish or self-defeating. It is simply allowing you to give yourself the love that you most likely have not been able to give yourself.

While the concept of self-love sounds like it should be easy, it often is a difficult process that requires you to seek many of the things that you seek from others from yourself.

Self-love requires:
- Self-validation
- Change of Environment
- Focusing on the Now
- *Self-care*

Self-Validation

"I am somebody." We have all heard the words of the Reverend Jessie Jackson, Sr. ringing in our ears at one time in our lives or another. The term self-validation is exactly this. Knowing that you are worthy of love, liberty and fulfillment of your dreams.

Many of us are guilty of requiring the validation of other people. These people may include parents, family, friends, teachers, bosses, etc. While it is good to hear that you are worthy out of the mouths of others, imagine how it will feel if your validation came from you. The term validation means having the acknowledgement or confirmation that an individual or their outlooks or feelings are worthwhile and valuable.

What happens if the person that you are seeking validation from is unable, unavailable, or simply cannot affirm your feelings, opinions, or emotions? Does this mean that these things are not valid?

Self-Validation Exercise:

List emotions, feelings, or situations that you have experienced that you feel require validation.

Example: I feel that I am deserving of a new job.
Then explain to yourself why this statement is valid.
Example: I feel that I am deserving of a new job because I have mastered all the skills necessary at my current position and seek growth.

Statement:

_____
_____
_____
_____
_____
_____

This is valid because:

_____
_____
_____
_____
_____

Statement:

_____
_____
_____
_____
_____

This is valid because:

_____
_____

Statement:

This is valid because:

Statement:

This is valid because:

Change of Environment

Environment plays a large role in how we perceive ourselves. While it may not be possible to simply pick up and leave an environment, we can change the ways in which we view environments or avoid specified environments altogether.

An example of an environments that are hard to change are extended family functions. While we may enjoy family functions we may not enjoy the behaviors of some family members within the function.

Example: Aunt Jackie has a habit of "telling it like it is." It appears that at every family function she gets into an altercation with someone over something that's usually not her business. These altercations often occur after she's had one drink too many. Family members usually make excuses for her saying things like, "You know how Jackie is." It has gotten so bad that the family expects everyone to just "toughen up" or "have a thicker skin."

How to you prepare for Auntie Jackie?

Remind yourself that no one has the right to steal your joy. Also, remind yourself that you have the right to your happiness.

Do you:
   a. Avoid all family functions where Aunt Jackie will be present?
   b. Go to the functions and avoid Aunt Jackie?
   c. Prepare a response to Aunt Jackie?
   d. Reply to Jackie the way she responds to you?

Correct response: C. Prepare a response to Aunt Jackie. Use this response if you become a part of her shenanigans.

Here is an example: *"This is a great party. It feels great to be around family. I do not want to discuss this subject at this time."* Repeat yourself if you must then continue enjoying yourself. This may require that you leave the room or engage in another activity.

You may ask yourself, "Why do I always have to be the bigger person?" The answer is simple. Because you *are* the bigger person. You are bigger than the circumstance and most important, you deserve happiness. If more family members respond to

Jackie in this manner then she may check her own behaviors. Fighting with her will only make it worse. Engaging in the dysfunction only brings more dysfunction.

An example of environments that are easy to change are jobs in some cases or an activity that no longer brings you joy.

Example: You and your girlfriends go out every Friday night. You go to a local club, have cocktails, and listen to music. You know that every time you and these ladies go out in this atmosphere, something negative happens.

Remind yourself that no one has the right to steal your joy. Also, remind yourself that you have the right to your happiness.

Do you:
    A. Go anyway because these ladies are your ride or dies?
    B. Go and drink less?
    C. Ignore the group text?
    D. Say no, and ask your friends to consider a new thing to do?

Correct response is D. At this point you are all clubbed out. If you and your friends have established healthy relationships they may be responsive to your suggestion to having a paint night or having brunch. Remember friendships, like relationships, add to you; they should not take anything away from you. Sure, you are ready to ride, but why do you have to die? Living and enjoying sounds so much better! If your friends go without you, that's fine. Don't risk your happiness to preserve something that does not bring you joy.

Focusing on the Now

Self-love also requires focusing on the now. This term means that you are present in the current moment. Staying in the moment allows you to focus on the things that you can change. What we know for certain is that the past is history and tomorrow is not promised. All we can control is the here and now.

Do not let your past mistakes prevent your present accomplishments. Use the past as a set of life lessons that can assist you in the prevention of making the same mistakes. Don't let yesterday's mistakes prevent you from trying to achieve a better you. I heard someone once say that they had no regrets in life, only life lessons. I can't promise that you won't regret things. I can promise that with every mistake you have the opportunity to learn and grow. Past failures do not make you a failure, they make you human.

No Regrets in Life, Only Life Lessons Exercise:

Look at the things in your life that you consider failures, accidents, or mistakes. Now list at least three (3) things that you learned from those situations.

This one is a hard one, so I will give a personal example:

Situation: At age 25, I let my then boyfriend drive my car my brand-new car (Yes, this happened for real). It was fresh off the lot and still had that new car smell. It was my first car. As we cruised down the street with the sunroof opened it happened. Someone hit my car. It happened in the blink of an eye. My car was totaled. My then boyfriend jumped ship and requested that I take the blame for the accident. The other driver was at fault and had no car insurance. This left me with a total loss of my car, and I had to purchase another car. He did not help me, and the insurance only paid out the current value of the car. This left me to not only pay the cost of the remaining car loan for that car, but the entire amount of the new car. Yes, I was "upside down" on my car loan.

What I learned:
1. Question anyone's car insurance before allowing someone to drive my vehicle.
2. Never let just a boyfriend drive my car.
3. Always purchase gap insurance.
4. Never admit fault for something I did not do even if love is involved.
5. A person who loves me will not ask me to risk my livelihood to save theirs.
6. Always have a great insurance plan that covers vehicle rental.

Complete your exercise without judgement. The goal is to reflect on what you learned.

Situation:
_____
_____
_____
_____

_____
_____
_____
_____

What I learned:

1._____
_____

2._____
_____

3._____
_____

4._____
_____

5._____
_____

Situation:

_____
_____
_____
_____
_____
_____

What I learned:

1._____
_____

2._____
_____

3._____
_____

4._____
_____

5._____
_____

Situation:
_____
_____
_____
_____
_____

What I learned:
1._____
_____
2._____
_____
3._____
_____
4._____
_____
5._____
_____

Self-Care

Lastly, self-love requires self-care. Being a better you requires doing the things that you need to be happy. I hope this book has given you the proper tools to seek out what makes you happy.

You do not need an excuse to love you. You are your excuse. Self-love is a journey not a destination. As you progress through life, you will continue to learn more, grow more and do more.

Take time to reflect on what you have learned about yourself after the completion of this workbook.

Self-Reflection Exercise:

About the Author

Dr. Michae' Wiley-Edgecombe' is a mental health clinician, advocate, and author. Dr. Wiley-Edgecombe' enjoys promoting self-love with the goal of growth and wellness. Within her practice, she uses a client-centered, solution-focused approach when assisting individuals in need. She is a specialist in motivational interviewing, substance use disorders and self-love.

Dr. Wiley-Edgecombe' is an advocate. In addition to clinical practices, she also provides consultation for program planning, implementation, and evaluation. It is her life's goal to be a change agent for those that she encounters.

Her motto that she lives by is: Be strong enough to feel.

www.ingramcontent.com/pod-product-compliance
Lightning Source LLC
Chambersburg PA
CBHW081421080526
44589CB00016B/2620